The Poodle

Shirley Walne

John Bartholomew & Son Limited
Edinburgh and London

The Publisher wishes to thank The Kennel Club and The American Kennel Club for permission to reproduce the breed standards.

First published in Great Britain 1977 by
JOHN BARTHOLOMEW & SON LIMITED
12 Duncan Street, Edinburgh EH9 1TA
And at 216 High Street, Bromley BR1 1PW

ISBN 0 7028 1064 9

1st edition

Prepared for the Publisher by Youé & Spooner Ltd. Colour illustrations by Charles Rush; airbrush drawings by Malcolm Ward

Printed in Great Britain by John Bartholomew & Son Limited

Contents

Preface

So gay and vivacious a dog as the Poodle has always attracted many admirers throughout its long history. Not least among these is the author of this book who shares her enthusiasm for the breed in all its varieties with the reader. Poodles thrive on human companionship. Only then can their wit, charm, humour and intelligence be fully appreciated. The author offers a wealth of advice from her long association with the breed, as a highly successful exhibitor, as an international judge, and as a connoisseur of the Poodle as a companion and family friend. Here you can not only learn about the physical requirements of the breed but also how to deal with the wiles of a clever dog intent on cajoling you into doing what it wants rather than what you want. The charm and sagacity of this favourite breed shine clearly in these pages and can only serve to increase their popularity.

Wendy Boorer
Consultant Editor

Introduction

There are not many breeds which have three sizes to their credit as does the Poodle, with the Standard, the Miniature and the Toy. There are not many breeds with so many colours which can range from coal black to shades of pale grey, known as silver; from deep orange, known as apricot, down to palest cream; from chocolate brown to café-au-lait; and last, of course, the pure white. When one's adored Poodle has died, one does not have to suffer from looking at the next puppy and expecting the same characteristics. One can have another colour and make a fresh start.

Poodles, no matter which size, love human companionship as much if not more than that of their own kind, and have the habit of 'taking over' the entire household. In appearance the Poodle has come down through the ages almost unchanged. It has been owned by kings, princes, statesmen and soldiers and has distinguished itself on the battlefield. It loves to clown and likes nothing better than to laugh with its master. The breed has been a sporting one from its early days. The dog is a great swimmer and was used in duck shooting. The Poodle will herd sheep, retrieve game and be a house pet. It loves to do tricks and there are very few indeed who dislike the show ring.

Having said all these things, it is obvious that I myself am addicted to Poodles. Nevertheless, not everyone can cope with the breed. They are extremely intelligent dogs and unless one has plenty of time to train them and give them something to do, there is no point in having a Poodle, no matter what age one is. They need human companionship and do not appreciate being shut up all day while their owners go out to work. If left alone like that they will soon find something to do to amuse themselves, often with disastrous results! Added to this, the Poodle is an expensive dog to keep because of the amount of clipping and trimming it requires.

Breed history

There are many differences of opinion as to the origin of the Poodle. The French declare the breed originated in France, but Russia and Germany claim the breed as well. It seems fairly certain that the Poodle's lion trim came from France. There is a print of 1771, called *The Dog Barbers,* showing a Poodle being trimmed, while others await their turns. A later print of 1881 shows two French women trimming Poodles. In another picture, King George IV, while still Prince Regent, can be seen sitting with his Poodle. In fact there are numerous prints and paintings showing Poodles with notable people from at least as early as 1529.

Most of the Poodles at this time were about 16-18in. (40-46cm.). It is later that one begins to see the Standard and the Miniature separate. Finally, in 1957, the Toy Poodle was recognised.

Originally Poodles were used largely for sport, and were generally either all black or all white. However there also existed particolours, where the main colour was white with either black or brown markings. These were never accepted by the Kennel Club for exhibition which I feel sure was a good thing, as they would soon have become mismarked rather than particoloured. There are still a few to be seen but they are not encouraged. In the past they were used mainly for truffle hunting, as apparently they had a keener sense of smell than the whole colours.

The sizes of the Poodle vary considerably from country to country. In England the Toy Poodle is up to 11in. (28cm.) and the Miniature up to 15in. (38cm.). The Standard Poodle can be any height from 15in. (38cm.) upward, but few under 20in. (50cm.) in height go far in the show ring. In fact, it is difficult to buy one smaller. Measuring is done from the top of the shoulder blade to the ground. One can obtain a measuring hoop which goes over the shoulders but care must be taken to ensure that the top goes over the shoulder blades and not just behind. A difference of up to 1in. (2.5cm.) can result if the hoop is not correctly positioned.

American Toys must not be more than 10in. (25cm.) in height, the Miniatures and the Standards having the same heights as the British although the former start from 10in. (25cm.). On the continent of Europe there are different sizes

POINTS OF THE POODLE

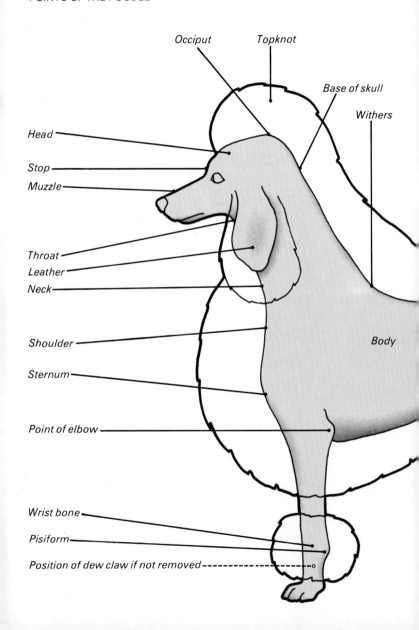

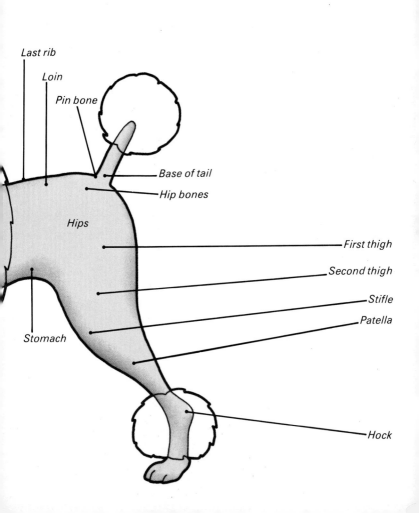

Last rib

Loin

Pin bone

Base of tail

Hip bones

Hips

First thigh

Second thigh

Stifle

Patella

Stomach

Hock

again. Their Toys are up to 35cm. (14in.), their Miniatures from 35-45cm. (14-18in.), and their Standards must not be more than 55cm. (22in.). So it can be seen how difficult it is from one country to another when none of them will agree regarding the ideal size. However, this does not really matter. A Poodle is a Poodle whatever the size!

In Germany a black Poodle must always be mated to a black, a white to a white, and so on. In America and Britain the colours can be mixed at will and it is from this mixing that the beautiful shades we see today have been produced. At one point this was to the detriment of the black Poodles whose coal black look became a rather dirty, muddy colour. But then breeders were more concerned with make, shape and personality than with colour. Nowadays there are numerous black bred blacks to be had, particularly in Miniatures.

Corded Poodle exhibited at the end of the nineteenth century

The breed standard

The British Standard

The Poodle standard in Britain is not so clearly defined as that of some other breeds, so some explanation is necessary.

'Characteristics and general appearance *That of a very active, intelligent, well balanced and elegant-looking dog with good temperament, carrying himself very proudly.'* This is an admirable description for which to aim but one must be careful of the snags. If too much importance is placed on *'carrying himself very proudly'* one is liable to breed a straight upper arm which gives a Poodle that extra proud carriage when moving, but also makes for weak shoulder joints and bad movement in front.

'Gait *Sound, free movements and light gait are essential.'* The difference here between light and heavy gait is the difference in movement between a hackney pony and a cart horse. *'Free'* means moving easily from the hips and shoulders, giving a dog that can cover a lot of ground in each stride.

'Head and Skull *Long and fine with slight peak at the back; the skull not broad and with a moderate stop; foreface strong and well chiselled, not falling away under the eyes. Bones and muscles flat; lips tight fitting; chin well defined but not protruding. The whole head must be in proportion to the size of the dog.'* One does not want the head to be so fine that it is too delicate to balance with the body. The *'slight peak'* at the back is the occipital bone. The *'moderate stop'* is the indentation between the eyes without which we would have a Collie or Bull Terrier type face which is quite alien to the Poodle. *'Well chiselled'* means that one should be able to see the bone structure and the veins just as though they had been artistically shaped with a chisel, so that there is no sudden disappearance of structure under the eyes. One does sometimes still see loose-fitting lips giving a slight houndy appearance and spoiling the expression.

'Eyes *Almond shaped, dark, not set too close together, full of fire and intelligence.'* *'Almond eyes'*, meaning oval in shape, are not so easily found in Toy Poodles. However, British Toys today have much better eye shape than they did. *'Dark'* does not mean black but rather a darkish brown or even a dark reddish brown colour. The eyes should never be yellow or green. Brown Poodles are allowed a lighter, amber coloured

Comparative sizes of the three varieties

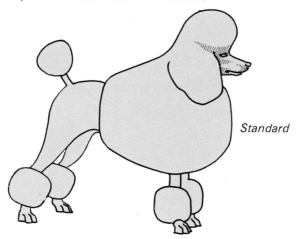

Standard

Miniature

Toy

eye, and so are the liver pointed apricots. However, most apricot Poodles one sees today have black points, meaning that the lips, eye rims and nose are black rather than brown.

'**Mouth** *Teeth, white and strong with a scissor bite. A full set of 42 teeth is desirable.*' Note the use of the word *'desirable'* here. It is not a heinous fault to be lacking any but one must always try to breed for the full set. Who wants a dog with only a few teeth?

'**Neck** *Well proportioned, of good length and strong, to admit of the head being carried high and with dignity, skin fitting tightly at the throat.*' The last phrase should be heeded, for it is so easy to breed Poodles that have loose skin in the area of the throat.

'**Forequarters** *Shoulders – strong and muscular, sloping well to the back, legs set straight from the shoulders, well muscled.*' This description is a little misleading where it speaks of *'legs set straight from the shoulders'.* In the dog the shoulder is formed by the shoulder blade and the humerus, often called the upper arm. The legs consist of the radius and ulna. The shoulder blade and humerus both need to slope back at an angle of 45 degrees, thus meeting in the front at an angle of 90 degrees. The elbow of the dog should be situated vertically below the top of the shoulder blade.

'**Body** *Chest – deep and moderately wide. Ribs – well sprung and rounded. Back – short, strong, slightly hollowed, loins broad and muscular.*' One will sometimes see a judge press down on a Poodle's back in order to ascertain how *'well sprung'* it is. One can soon tell if the dog is roach-backed or not, even if it has been so well trimmed as to hide it! It is difficult, in this day and age, for most people to give their Poodles sufficient exercise for them to develop the muscular loins required by the standard. However a Poodle lacking in muscle will never move as well as one which is well muscled up.

'**Hindquarters** *Thighs well developed and muscular, well bent stifles, well let down hocks, hind legs turning neither in nor out.*' The *'well bent stifles'* means that one should not be able to draw a vertical line from hip joint to toes when the dog is standing. The Poodle's body should be able to fit into a square with its head out one side and the hind legs out the other from the stifle joint downwards. At the other extreme the Poodle does not want an exaggerated stance so that it looks as though it is about to kneel down. When this happens it is usually a sign that the femur is too short, with the tibia and fibula growing too long to counteract this. *'Well let down hocks'* really means well bent hocks which ensure good propulsion when moving. Hind legs can and do turn in and out in some cases. This is a bad fault, due either to bad rearing or to an hereditary condition.

'Feet *Pastern strong, tight feet proportionally small, oval in shape, turning neither in nor out, toes arched, pads thick and hard, well cushioned.'* In most cases feet are an inherited condition whether they be good or bad. Although one is told that lack of exercise on hard ground can cause flat, soft feet, in fact, if a foot is made incorrectly nothing on earth will alter it. Front feet tend to turn out if the Poodle is narrowly built. Also, if the shoulders are wrongly constructed, you can be pretty certain the elbows will be turning outwards and the feet turning inwards. A big coat can cover a multitude of sins, so it is up to the judge to find them out.

Skeleton of the Poodle

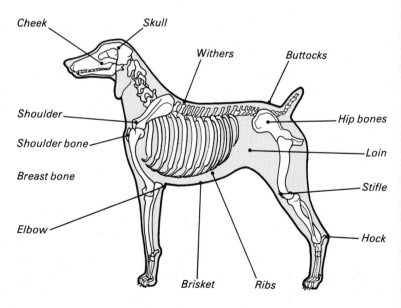

Cheek   Skull   Withers   Buttocks

Shoulder   Hip bones

Shoulder bone   Loin

Breast bone   Stifle

Elbow   Hock

Brisket   Ribs

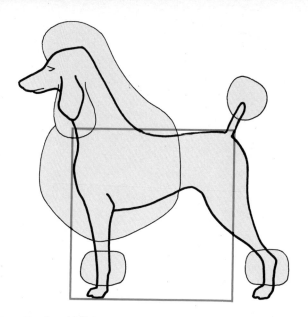

The Poodle should fit into a square

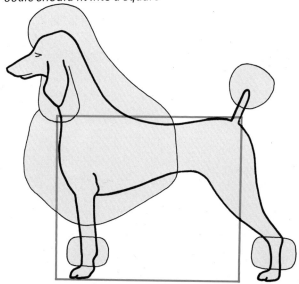

The top illustration shows correct proportions; the lower Poodle is too long in back

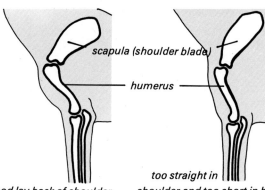

scapula (shoulder blade)

humerus

good lay back of shoulder

too straight in shoulder and too short in humerus

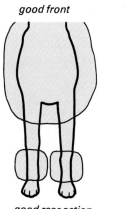

good front

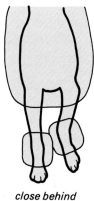

dishing in front

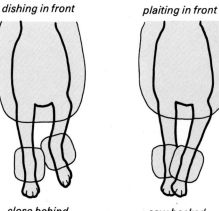

plaiting in front

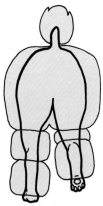

good rear action

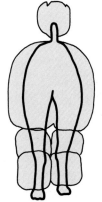

close behind

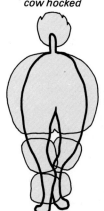

cow hocked

16

'**Tail** *Set on rather high, well carried at a slight angle away from the body, never curled or carried over the back, thick at the root.*' If one thinks of the hands of a clock showing five minutes past twelve, the minute hand shows the correct angle from the vertical of a Poodle's tail carriage.

'**Coat** *Very profuse and dense of good harsh texture without knots and tangles. All short hair close, thick and curly. It is strongly recommended that the traditional clip be adhered to.*' It is the number of hairs to the inch that counts rather than the length. Above all, the texture is important. If the texture is correct, all the short hair is automatically curly. One sees from time to time lacquer being sprayed on to coats; this is completely against British Kennel Club rules. All grease, lacquer, colour, rinse, dye, etc. is forbidden under Rule 17. Anyone found to be using them may be disqualified. Tests are occasionally made at shows by the Kennel Club. Anyone suspecting that a dog is dyed may, on payment of a fee, make a complaint to the Secretary of the show, and appropriate action will then be taken.

'**Colour** *All solid colours. White and cream Poodles to have black nose, lips and eye rims, black toenails desirable. Brown Poodles to have dark amber eyes, dark liver nose, lips, eye rims and toenails. Apricot Poodles to have dark eyes with black points or deep amber eyes with liver points. Black, silver, and blue Poodles to have black nose, lips, eye rims and toenails. Cream, apricot, brown, silver, and blue Poodles may show varying shades of the same colour up to 18 months. Clear colours preferred.*'

'**Size** *15 in. (38 cm.) and over.*'

'**Faults** *Heavy build, clumsiness, long back, snipy in foreface, light or round or prominent eyes, lippiness, bad carriage, heavy gait, coarse head, over- or under-shot or pincer mouth, flesh coloured nose, coarse legs and feet, long flat toes, open soft coats with no curl, particolours – white markings on black or coloured poodles, lemon or other markings on white poodles, vicious temperament.*' Note – male animals should have two apparently normal testicles fully descended into the scrotum.

'**Poodle Miniature** *The Poodle Miniature should be in every respect a replica in miniature of the Poodle Standard. Height at shoulder should be under 15 in. (38 cm.) but not under 11 in. (28 cm.).*

Poodle Toy *The standard of the Poodle Toy is the same as that* *of the Poodle Standard and the Poodle Miniature except that the height at shoulder should be under 11 in. (28 cm.).'*

It has recently been decided by the British Kennel Club that oversize Miniatures and oversize Toy Poodles may be shown, and that it is a fault not a disqualification as it was in the past. It is, therefore, up to the judge to decide if an oversized exhibit is a more serious fault than an exhibit with, say, a faulty mouth or incorrect shoulder placement. Personally, I would prefer to put up an oversized Poodle, if it were sound and free from any other major fault, rather than an untypical, unsound specimen. But I would think twice before giving it top honours! Continually breeding and showing oversized dogs would soon mean that the Toy and Miniature Poodle would no longer exist.

For the time being in Britain, one may still interbreed Miniature and Toy Poodles. This is to enable type to be established in the Toy Poodle. It takes at least thirty years to establish a size and type but the time will soon come when the two breeds will be finally separated and one will not be allowed to interbreed at all.

Care must be taken when breeding the tiny ones that one knows and understands what is behind their pedigree. A small Toy bitch could well have had a Miniature dam of up to 15in. (38cm.). Similarly, the sire could have had one or two Miniature grandparents. Always be sure to take advice from the breeder of both sire and dam before mating a bitch. Although a bitch can have a caesarian operation with perfect safety, no one wants to establish a breed which cannot have puppies naturally.

When selling Toy puppies, I would never recommend anyone to guarantee the size. One could be in legal difficulties if a Toy Poodle grew oversize.

The American Standard

The American standard for the Poodle is rather more explicit than the British. The breed of Poodle is divided into three varieties: Standard, 15in. (38cm.) or over at the shoulder; Miniature, under 15in. (38cm.) but over 10in. (25cm.) at the shoulder; Toy, 10in. (25cm.) or under at the shoulder.

'General Appearance, Carriage and Condition *That of a very active, intelligent and elegant-looking dog, squarely built, well-proportioned, moving soundly and carrying himself proudly. Properly clipped in the traditional fashion and carefully groomed, the Poodle has about him an air of* distinction and dignity peculiar to himself.

Head and Expression a) Skull: moderately rounded, with a slight but definite stop. Cheek-bones and muscles flat. Muzzle: long, straight and fine, with slight chiseling under the eyes. Strong without lippiness. The chin definite enough to preclude snipiness. Teeth white, strong and with a scissors bite. Nose sharp with well-defined nostrils. b) Eyes: set far apart, very dark, full of fire and intelligence, oval in appearance. c) Ears: set low and hanging close to the head. The leather should be long, wide and heavily feathered.

Neck and Shoulders Neck well proportioned, strong and long to admit of the head being carried high and with dignity. Skin snug at throat. The neck should rise from strong muscular shoulders which slope back from their point of angulation at the upper foreleg to the withers.

Body The chest deep and moderately wide. The ribs well sprung and braced up. The back short, strong and slightly hollowed, the loins short, broad and muscular. (Bitches may be slightly longer in back than dogs.)

Tail Straight, set on rather high, docked but of sufficient length to ensure a balanced outline. It should be carried up and in a gay manner.

Legs The forelegs straight from the shoulder, parallel and with bone and muscle in proportion to size of dog. The pasterns should be strong. The hind legs very muscular, stifles well bent and hocks well let down. The thigh should be well developed, muscular and showing width in the region of the stifle to insure strong and graceful action. The four feet should turn neither in nor out. Feet – rather small and oval in shape. Toes arched, close and cushioned on thick, hard pads.

Coat Quality; very profuse, of harsh texture and dense throughout.

Clip A Poodle may be shown in the "Puppy" clip or in the traditional "Continental" clip or the "English Saddle" clip. A Poodle under a year old may be shown in the "Puppy" clip with the coat long except the face, feet and base of tail, which should be shaved. Dogs one year old or older must be shown in either the "Continental" clip or "English Saddle" clip.

In the "Continental" clip the hindquarters are shaved with pompoms on hips (optional). The face, feet, legs and tail are shaved leaving bracelets on the hind legs, puffs on the forelegs and a pompom on the end of the tail. The rest of the body must be left in full coat.

A white Miniature Poodle
Mrs Rose's Ch. Stanlyn Cleopatra

Champions of the 1970's

A white Standard Poodle
Miss Willis' Ch. Bibelot's Polar de la Fontaine

A black Miniature Poodle
Mrs P. Howard Price's Ch. Mickey Finn of Montfleuri

Champions of the 1970's

Toy Poodles

An apricot
Miss V. Ferguson's Ch. Contecrest D'Orcot Saffron

A black
Miss Willis' Springett Mr Perkins

In the "English Saddle" clip the hindquarters are covered with a short blanket of hair except for a curved shaved area on the flank and two shaved bands on each hind leg. The face, feet, forelegs and tail are shaved leaving puffs on the forelegs and a pompom at the end of the tail. The rest of the body must be left in full coat.

Color The coat must be an even and solid color at the skin. In blues, greys, silvers, browns, café-au-laits, apricots and creams the coat may show varying shades of the same color. This is frequently present in the somewhat darker feathering of the ears and in the tipping of the ruff. While clear colors are definitely preferred such natural variation in the shading of the coat is not to be considered a fault. Brown and café-au-lait

A blue Poodle

Poodles have liver-colored noses, eye rims and lips, dark toe-nails and dark amber eyes. Black, blue, grey, silver, apricot, cream and white Poodles have black noses, eye rims and lips, black or self-colored toenails and very dark eyes. In the apricots while black is preferred, liver-colored noses, eye-rims and lips, self-colored toenails and amber eyes are permitted but are not desirable.

Gait *A straightforward trot with light springy action. Head and tail carried high. Forelegs and hind legs should move parallel turning neither in nor out. Sound movement is essential.*

Size

Standard *The Standard Poodle is over 15 in. (38 cm.) at the withers. Any Poodle which is 15 in. (38 cm.) or less in height shall be disqualified from competition as a Standard Poodle.*

Miniature *The Miniature Poodle is 15 in. (38 cm.) or under at the withers, with a minimum height in excess of 10 in. (25 cm.). Any Poodle which is over 15 in. (38 cm.), or 10 in. (25 cm.) or less at the withers shall be disqualified from competition as a Miniature Poodle.*

Toy *The Toy Poodle is 10 in. (25 cm.) or under at the withers. Any Poodle which is more than 10 in. 25 cm.) at the withers shall be disqualified from competition as a Toy Poodle.*

Value of Points

General appearance, carriage and condition	20
Head, ears, eyes and expression	20
Neck and shoulders	10
Body and tail	15
Legs and feet	15
Coat – color and texture	10
Gait	10
Total	100

Major Faults *Eyes: round in appearance, protruding, large or very light. Jaws: undershot, overshot or wry mouth. Cowhocks. Feet: flat or spread. Tail: set low, curled or carried over the back. Shyness.*

Disqualifications *Particolors: the coat of a particolored dog is not an even solid color at the skin but is variegated in patches of two or more colors. Any type of clip other than those listed in section on coat. Any size over or under the limits specified in section on size.'*

Choosing a puppy

If you are choosing a pet puppy, the first question is, which size? The Toy is ideal for the person who has no car and for someone who likes a little dog, though this does not mean that the Toy does not want exercise and freedom. A Toy Poodle likes a good walk daily. It is just as much of a sporting dog as the other sizes if it is allowed to be. Do not, however, be browbeaten into taking it, or its bigger brethren, for a walk at the same time each day. Once you have done this for a few days running you will find yourself being bullied. All Poodles seem to have an inbuilt clock and know exactly what time everything should be done for them.

Do not buy a Toy Poodle thinking it will be cheaper to feed. Toy Poodles are often a bit more particular than their bigger brothers. They prefer a steak to the cheaper cuts of meat, chicken to fish, etc. If you have decided to give the dog steak one day, it may very well do its best to stop eating until it gets steak again, which can be a great worry in an animal of which you are fond. Though one often hears 'Oh, let him starve, he'll eat when he wants to', this is not always the case, as Toy Poodles can be very determined. Their likes and dislikes can be expensive.

Miniatures, too, can be this way inclined but Standards generally can be relied upon to eat a normal diet of biscuit meal, tinned meats and most of the usual dog foods. Unlike the Toy, the Standard Poodle does not usually get the idea of missing a meal in case there is something better coming along later. On the whole, Toys are not as delicate as one might think from their size, but being bred down has had its own problems, especially from the show point of view.

When buying a pet, go for a sturdy little dog, the one which does not necessarily have all the show points required. Do not fall for the shy, nervous one which sits in a corner or under a chair. Never buy one which, the moment you put your hand near, immediately shies away or snaps at you. Such an animal may become the most devoted dog possible but, when the day comes that you are ill or going abroad and it has to go into a boarding kennel or to stay with friends, then not only will the dog suffer but you will also. Always make sure you can see at least one parent, preferably the mother. One can tell a lot from her as to what the puppy will be like. If you are not sure, take someone with you who has the knowledge. Never buy from a dirty or smelly kennel. You can be sure that you will arrive home from there with a puppy full of worms, lice or even with a skin infection, so do go to a reliable breeder of Poodles. This is more important still where Toy Poodles are concerned as, without being delicate or weedy, they do not have the stamina of the bigger sizes.

The next size up, the Miniature, is a lovely dog to have as a pet if you feel you cannot cope with a Standard and do not want a Toy. It will fit in anywhere and does not take up a great deal of room. It is a bit too heavy to carry far, as you can the Toy, but it is a tough chap and a convenient size to be lifted with ease on to buses and trains. The same rules apply here regarding purchase. Make sure you go to a sensible breeder who knows what he is breeding and hasn't just found a dog round the corner for the sire. Character is so important that I put that before anything. As in the other sizes, there are nervous dogs around. Don't buy one, as they are a constant worry. There is also the very sensitive type of dog, which again can be troublesome. Poodles do not suffer any more than other breeds from these defects of temperament but the Poodle, no matter what size, should be a healthy, confident, intelligent and clever dog.

The Standard is a big dog needing good feeding. It will eat a lot as a puppy and needs it to grow up to be a healthy dog, so you should make sure you have the time and money to spend on a Standard Poodle.

No matter which size they are, all Poodles need to be trimmed at least once in eight weeks, or better still every six weeks. This is an added expense compared with other breeds. However, there is the advantage that there are no hairs left on the furniture. Not having to have the furniture cleaned and the chair covers laundered so frequently does compensate somewhat for the added expense of trimming. Needless to say, it is more expensive to have a Standard trimmed than a Toy, although the Standard is easier in many ways. Somehow the Toys often object more to the process than the Miniatures or the Standards. But each individual has its likes and dislikes, as I have said before, and it all adds to their enchantment.

Most breeders let their puppies go at eight weeks, although in some cases it is wiser to leave Toy puppies with their mother up to ten weeks of age. The Toys have only small litters, from one to five puppies. Miniatures can have as many as eight or nine, but five or six is more usual. Standard litters can be up to fourteen in number but most breeders will not allow the mother to bring up more than eight or nine. This is plenty for any bitch to rear. Usually, by eight weeks of age, the Standard Poodle mother is glad to see the back of her pups.

To find a Poodle breeder one can contact the Kennel Club. The British Kennel Club is at 1-4 Clarges Street, Piccadilly, London WIY 8AB. The American Kennel Club is at 51, Madison Avenue, New York, N.Y. 10010. Though often not prepared to recommend individual breeders, the Kennel Club will certainly be able to give details of a Poodle Club in your area and the secretary of this can give further information. A friend who has a pure-bred puppy of any breed could give you the address of where he obtained his dog and this breeder might very well be able to put you in touch with a Poodle kennel. A veterinary surgeon could give you some kennel names too. There are also periodicals published giving details of shows and listing puppies for sale. In Britain there are two weekly magazines, *Our Dogs* and *Dog World.* In America there is a monthly publication, *Pure-Bred Dogs.*

When you have decided which puppy it is to be and where it is to come from, try to see the puppy at six weeks of age and obtain a diet sheet and advice from the breeder, so that you will have everything ready for the great day. You may find that you have to wait two or three months before collecting the puppy of your choice, but do be patient. Don't just rush out and buy any old puppy.

Colour too needs consideration. It may be that you have an elderly relative living with you and a lighter colour would be more practical, so that the dog can easily be seen. Do not worry about a lighter colour looking dirtier more quickly. This is not really true as all the colours can look equally dirty. As long as the dog is groomed and trimmed regularly, you can never be accused of having a dirty animal.

Strangely enough, the colours do have their own characteristics. In Standards we find apricots are perhaps more highly strung than the other colours. I would add that this is not always the case and I can think of a number of apricots which are solid, sensible Poodles. Silvers are inclined to 'do' and think afterwards and similarly with the apricots, whereas blacks and browns think first. Standard whites are more

Many Poodles change in colour as they mature

sensitive, though this generalisation does not necessarily include the other two sizes. I think in all cases the blacks are the most popular, with whites coming second. Again this does not mean you should rush out and buy a black. Any good breeder will give you all the details of character from the puppies, parentage and advise on the most suitable for you.

When the day comes for collection, take newspaper and a couple of towels in case the puppy is travel sick and, if it is a long journey, take a bowl and a bottle of water. The puppy will need lots of encouragement in all it does and to be given confidence, for the Poodle is not a breed which dashes into all and sundry. It likes to think things out for itself, especially if it is an older puppy which has never been outside the kennel before. Incidentally, should you have decided to purchase an older puppy or even an adult dog, never fuss over it. Let it come to you and give it time to think things out. Remember your own first days at school and how very strange everything was. This applies very much to the older Poodle in new surroundings. A baby puppy will usually be far too interested in when its next meal is coming to bother about the difference. In all probability the eight-week-old baby will not have met a collar and lead yet but it is as well to take one with you. Put it on before getting back into the car. The dog may want to relieve itself on the way home and one cannot let it out of the car without a lead.

It is always a good thing to have a child's play pen or a puppy play pen. A child's play pen can be lined with wire netting to prevent the puppy getting out between the bars, or getting stuck as in the case of the Standard. Preferably this should be placed on a tiled floor which is heavily covered in newspaper. A cardboard box at one end makes a bed. The side should be cut down leaving a few inches so that a blanket placed inside will not fall out. Such a pen is useful for, in it, the puppy can be safely out of one's way and can fall asleep where it knows it will not be disturbed. Standard Poodles need much more rest than their two little brothers, as they have a lot of growing to do. The smaller sizes will be much keener to see what is going on and will appear to rush about more. The first night, unless it is a case of the puppy going to be allowed to sleep in one's bedroom, may be rather noisy, when the puppy discovers it has no mother, brothers or sisters. A stone hot water bottle, well wrapped up, will be a comfort and some people suggest

A suitable playpen

that a clock wrapped up so that the puppy can hear the ticking noise, also helps. A sedative from the veterinary surgeon is possibly the best answer. But whatever you decide, you should stick to it. Do not think it is a good idea to have the puppy in your room just for the first few nights. It is not!

Puppies need regular meals. Most breeders have their own methods and times of feeding which should be adhered to for at least a few weeks before altering to suit your own requirements. You will probably be given a day's food supply plus vitamin supplements when you collect your puppy. The following diet for an eight-week-old puppy is included as a guide only. The dog should be having four meals a day at this age.

8a.m. *Standard* ¼-½ pint (1½-3dl.) milk with 2 heaped tablespoonfuls of baby cereal; 1 heaped tablespoonful of honey or glucose added; puppy biscuits or baby rusks.

Miniature ¼ pint (1½dl.) milk with 1 tablespoonful of baby cereal; 1 dessertspoonful of honey or glucose added; puppy biscuits or baby rusks.

Toy Tiny dish with as much milk as required with 1 dessertspoonful of baby cereal and 1 teaspoonful of glucose or honey added; half a baby rusk or puppy biscuit.

Any cereal may be given as a change.

12 noon *Standard* 4-6oz. (125-175g.) cooked meat finely cut up or minced with 1 cupful of puppy meal which has previously been soaked; 1 or 2 slices of wholemeal bread plus suitable vitamins. Boned fish or boned chicken, ox cheek, tinned meat, tripe, etc. may be given as a change. Cooked rice, macaroni, pastry, etc. may be given as a change from the puppy meal.

Miniature 3oz. (75g.) cooked meat finely minced with half a cupful of puppy meal added; otherwise as for the Standard puppy in suitable quantity.

Toy 1 tablespoonful of finely minced meat with half a slice of wholemeal bread; otherwise as for the Standard puppy in suitable quantity plus, of course, vitamins.

4p.m. *All sizes* should have similar feeds to the 12 noon unless it is very hot when this feed should be given in the cool of the evening and the 8p.m. feed given at this time.

8p.m. *Standard* ½ pint (3dl.) milk preferably made into one of the proprietary milky drinks with glucose or honey added.

Miniature and Toy A similar milky drink in smaller quantity.

All sizes may have a scrambled or boiled egg for a change and biscuits to go to bed with. The Miniatures and Toys do really prefer plain sweet biscuits at this age (the ones suitable for humans), and all love their special chocolate drops.

From this it can be seen that when you bring home a puppy of eight weeks, you will need milk or milk powder, vitamins, meat and puppy meal. Don't forget to collect the pedigree and transfer certificate. You will also need a brush and comb. There are always new brushes and combs coming on the market and most breeders will help you in deciding which to use. Don't ask advice from dog shops unless you, or the shop owner, know exactly what you want. Trade stands at dog shows are one of the best places to buy equipment as the owners of these usually know what is best. It is wise to have your puppy's feet and tail trimmed at an early age and not to wait until it becomes a necessity at about five months. It is rather hard on a puppy at that age to be clipped for the first time, and also hard on the person who does the clipping. Always ask the trimmer to cut your puppy's nails and in particular to look at the dew claws, although in most cases these will have been removed.

If, when collecting your puppy, you discover it has a hernia, do not be too alarmed. This is often caused where the mother has chewed the umbilical cord too close when the puppy was born. Unless it is very big there is no need to worry but, if you are at all uneasy, do ask your veterinary surgeon. Sometimes a breeder may forget to mention it as it happens so frequently.

Now we must consider the show puppy. If you have been to

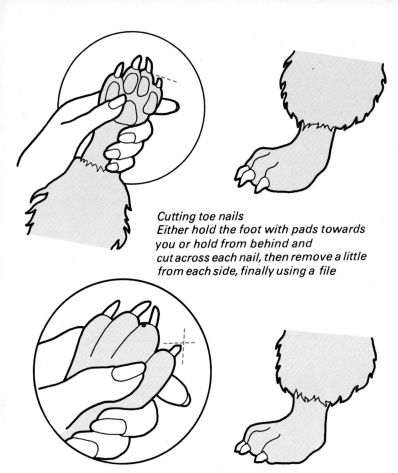

Cutting toe nails
Either hold the foot with pads towards
you or hold from behind and
cut across each nail, then remove a little
from each side, finally using a file

a number of shows you will have seen that showing entails a lot of hard work with long hours. If you are married with young children, then wait until they are grown up. Dog shows and children just do not go together unless you have plenty of help. One or the other has to suffer.

Although one wants a great character with an outgoing personality, it is the make and shape of the dog which is going to count in the show ring. The judge sees only what is in front of him and, although great showmanship is an advantage, character does not really come into it as such. First of all, consider the structure of the dog. Read the Poodle standard until you know it inside out. Although you will find the standard in this book, it may not always be convenient to have this with you. Copies of any breed standard can be obtained from the appropriate Kennel Club. (The Poodle is in the Utility group in Britain and the Non-sporting group in America.)

I find I like to choose my puppy at six weeks of age, no matter if it is a Standard, Miniature or Toy. The overall picture of a six-week-old puppy will be the overall picture when fully grown, bar accidents of course. Lack of permanent teeth and light eyes instead of the required dark ones – these things one has to wait for and hope that time will correct them. However, if one knows the breeding, one is pretty certain what to expect.

From eight weeks onward the puppy changes each week. The neck disappears and one is certain it will never come back again! The hindquarters are higher up one week and one is convinced that the front will never catch up. The feet go flat; the tail curls over; the nose goes snipy; and the legs go cowhocked. In fact, it can look as though one has the worst puppy that ever was born. But do not despair. When it is over six months old it will be worth looking at. By two years old it will be a real handsome guy and possibly a champion. My personal feeling is that a dog which is made a champion before it is two years old usually coarsens in the head, in fact coarsens all over, by the time it is three and a half years. However there are exceptions to this.

Again colour is important for the show dog. You can get away with more with a not so good pure white beautifully presented than you can with any other colour. However, the white's coat will need far more care than any other colour. Blacks always look good if they are well constructed, as do browns, but they are apt to fade in colour. Apricots are difficult in that they can fade too. Silvers and blues are the most difficult of all, owing to the slowness with which they change colour from the black they are born with. I would advise a black Poodle for a beginner in the show ring.

Before I say more, I must mention that if a beginner buys the most expensive, the most perfect puppy, or even a fully made up champion, he will not win with it unless the dog is properly prepared and presented. For this reason it is often better to employ a handler to prepare and show the dog for you. A handler is a person who has studied dogs all his life, enjoys showing, and spends his life preparing and handling all breeds. A few like to specialise but no matter which breed he handles, the professional has the knowledge of how best to present that dog in the show ring.

However, if you are determined to do it yourself, do not spend a lot of money on your first dog. Buy a reasonably good dog and you will learn together. It is not just a case of taking your dog into the ring. Even if it is already a champion, that dog is used to a certain person handling it in a certain way, and no two people handle alike. So buy a nice, good-looking dog and learn the ropes with it. Your second dog is the one with which you will really go places.

A silver Poodle

A blue Poodle

General care

The pet Poodle should not take any longer than any other breed to look well groomed and cared for. Every dog should have a good grooming daily. The pet Poodle of whatever size should be taught to be groomed on a table. It is essential that this has a non-slippery surface. Special tables can be obtained from most dog requisite firms. First stand your puppy on the table saying 'Stand', and then very gently pull all four feet towards you from under it, at the same time saying 'Lie down'. The Standard and the Miniature will usually co-operate quite quickly without any undue fuss. Keep saying 'Lie down' once the dog is still. Let it get up again at once but never take your hands off it in case the puppy panics and falls off. Be sure to say 'Up you get'. The Toy Poodle, being so small, can be allowed to stand or sit. It is inclined to get more upset than its two bigger brothers. For the first few days just teach the dog to lie on its side, even leaning over it a little to help persuade it even more. Once the animal is happy, gently rub its tummy and then gradually use a brush. As time goes on the dog can be persuaded to stay a little longer each day until eventually it will stay as long as you want. Use the same words and method each time and never let it get up without the command.

This method is such a help for the trimmer and will result in the Poodle being perfectly happy to have its feet clipped and its trousers groomed at any angle. Once you have got the puppy to relax on its side, you can then train it to stand. The trousers can now be groomed by starting at the feet and brushing a layer of hair all round. Gradually work your way to the top of the leg, a layer at a time.

Grooming depends so much on which trim you like for your Poodle. If you have very little time, then I would advise the sporting look with all the hair cut to about ½in. (1.2cm.) all over, a rounded top knot, a pompom on the tail and bracelets just above the feet. This looks neat and balanced. There is also the Dutch trim with large trousers all the way up the legs and the Kerry trim which has trousers not quite so high up the leg. Probably the most popular is the Lamb trim which has just narrow trousers, with the face, feet and tail clipped. Some like a moustache and beard left, others just a moustache. The advantage with pet Poodles is that one can have exactly what one wants.

High trousers for the Dutch trim which may or may not have whiskers, beard or a round topknot or graduated up from the neck

Kerry trim without feet trimmed

The red circle indicates alternative variations

The sporting trim

Ears with hair clipped off or with a tassel left

Toy Poodles are often easier to groom and clip sitting on one's lap. With the dog's back towards you brush and comb the trousers away from you, starting at the base of each leg and working upwards. Having groomed the trousers, brush and comb the body, followed by the ears, top knot and chest.

While grooming the ears, be sure to have a good look into them. One of the Poodle's weaknesses can be dirty ears. The long leathers covered with hair prevents the air from circulating in the ear which then becomes more liable to infection. Perhaps there is a little scratch which, before one knows it, causes a very sore ear. Clean the ears out occasionally with a small piece of cotton wool and then dust with boracic powder. There are numerous ear applications on the market but until one has had plenty of experience I advise a visit to the veterinary surgeon who will prescribe treatment for an infection. All sizes of Poodles as puppies have hair in their

41

Low Dutch trim on chocolate Poodle

Lamb trim on white Poodle

ears which can cause a lot of irritation if not removed. However, to take it out too soon, particularly with forceps, can cause a great deal of discomfort and pain. The best age to remove it seems to be around seven months, but like everything else it varies from dog to dog. The most suitable way is to apply a little ear powder into the ear and then, with finger and thumb, hold a very few hairs at one time and jerk the hair out quickly. The Poodle should suffer no pain at all. Continue to remove the hair until it has all been taken out. If the Poodle does complain, then either the hair is not ready for removal or you are pulling too many hairs at one time.

The Toy and Miniature Poodles suffer more from eye troubles than the Standards. It is possibly the construction of the tiny head of the Toy, and in some cases Miniatures too, which causes the eyes to run and inevitably one sees the brown stain marks just below the eye itself. So far as I know, there is no real solution to this problem but an occasional wash with an eye lotion or even warm milk will help. If it becomes really bad, a veterinary surgeon can prescribe a suitable ointment. There are, of course, various remedies which one can buy and which are worth trying.

Teeth also need care. Standards have little or no trouble at all. A show dog should have a full set of teeth, or at least all his incisors, eye teeth, etc. An occasional missing premolar in an otherwise good dog will not usually lose him a placing, though on the Continent this is taboo. All their dogs must have a full set or be disqualified. Teeth can be cleaned by brushing or scaling; the latter should be done by the trimmer or a veterinary surgeon. Providing that the dog has something hard to chew, it is not often it will have discoloured teeth. Miniatures do suffer a little this way and their teeth will need more cleaning, as often these dogs will not chew big beef bones or hard biscuits. The Toy is the worst of all in this respect and I have known some lose most of their teeth by the time they are eight years old or even younger. A periodical visit to the veterinary surgeon is advisable.

The teeth themselves should be level, with the top set just overlapping the lower ones. One does not want what are called undershot or overshot mouths, the former being when the lower protrude forward beyond the top set and the latter when the top set protrude well over the lower set. These faults were very prevalent in Toys and Miniatures at one time and

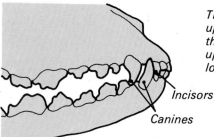

The correct 'scissors bite'. The upper incisors fit closely over the lower incisors and the upper canines fit behind the lower canines.

Incisors

Canines

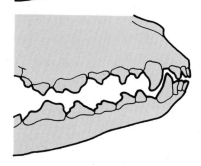

'Pincer' or 'Level bite'. Teeth of the upper jaw meet the teeth of the lower jaw.

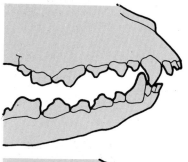

'Overshot'. The top jaw protrudes over the lower, causing a space. The canines are in reverse positions.

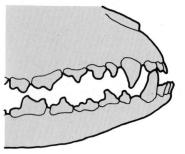

'Undershot'. The lower incisors protrude beyond the upper jaw, causing a space between the upper and lower canines.

still occasionally occur. In the Standards this is a fault that should not be bred from and, if very pronounced, it can cause difficulty in feeding. From the pet point of view, if the mouth is only just over or undershot, it has little significance and no effect whatsoever on the dog's health or character.

A Poodle, no matter what size, enjoys a jolly good run each day, but does not need to go for a five-mile walk. On no account take it in the road without a lead. No one is going to stand aside to let a dog pass by. It is the dog which goes into the road and gets run over. There are always temptations for a loose dog, such as a cat on the other side of the road which the dog feels must be investigated. If possible take it to a park, field or somewhere where it can run about loose with safety. Never let a Poodle, in fact any dog, go out on its own. There are too many dangers with traffic and livestock. Poodles have the most amazing memory and will never forget once they have found the delights of chasing sheep or chickens. One cannot blame a farmer complaining or even shooting your dog.

Another hazard to be considered are dog toys, particularly balls. The Miniatures and Toys are perfectly safe and happy to play with one the size of a tennis ball but a Standard needs a larger one. Never let a Standard catch a ball in its mouth. Poodles have been known to die having caught the ball which has lodged in their throats and choked them to death. A football is the size needed for a Standard. Pull toys are not very suitable. They can easily injure the teeth or pull them out of shape. Be careful that your dog cannot chew pieces from a favourite toy and swallow them.

A pet Poodle needs a good sized bed in a draught-free area, with frequent changes of blankets. Better still, it would like its own chair. All Poodles, no matter what size, like an armchair of their own and can jump sufficiently high to get into one. In fact, all three sizes can jump terrific heights and, when wiring one's garden, 6ft. (1.83m.) is none too high.

The show dog, providing it is also a pet, is equally happy to have its own bed in the house. However, if it is a bitch that is going to be bred from and one or two puppies kept, then one must think in terms of kennels, or a suitable outhouse which can be altered for the purpose. In many areas planning permission needs to be obtained before putting up a suitable kennel. So often breeding kennels start up without thought and before one has really considered it the house has become

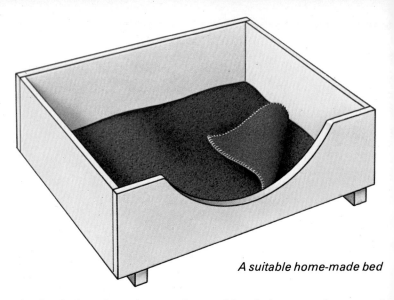

A suitable home-made bed

the kennel and one's non-doggy friends become fewer and fewer.

There are many establishments which make very good and suitable kennels. I would never advise anyone to buy a building and convert it unless they had a wide knowledge of appropriate materials. Personally I like a kennel which has a range of compartments with plenty of windows along the opposite side of the passage way. The kennel should be tall enough for the Poodle not to feel cramped, and have heat, light and radio installed. Each kennel for a Standard needs to be at least 5ft. 6in. by 8ft. (1.68m. by 2.44m.), so that the dog can have a companion and room to play. Miniatures and Toys can, of course, have smaller kennels but the bigger they are the more room they have to play. I am not in favour of cages or Poodles living separately just so that they grow a coat for the show ring. One hears sad tales of little dogs being confined to cages on the wall, piled on top of each other, with only a few moments allowed outside in a concrete run. I am sure God never meant his creatures to be kept under such conditions. One even hears of force-feeding to grow coat, which makes me ill even to think of it. It may be necessary for a very sick dog, but never for a supposedly fit show dog. On the whole Miniatures and Toys are not kennel dogs and do far better in the house.

Each Poodle needs its own bed in the kennels. Standards need something at least 2ft. 6in. (76cm.) square. A wooden floor is really more suitable for a growing puppy than concrete, which is not only damaging for bone development but is difficult to keep clean and free from smell.

Like all dogs, Poodles need training. There is really a basic snag, for it is actually the owner that needs teaching so that he knows how to train his dog. There are very many dog training clubs, most of which are booked up in advance. Few will accept puppies under the age of six months, by which time many Poodles will have learned a lot of bad habits. Though no puppy needs to have formal training before the age of six months, if the owner would go to classes to learn how to start the puppy off correctly in lead training, how to use the correct tone of voice, how to teach the puppy to come when called, a lot of training, or to be precise retraining, would not be necessary. Local training classes can be found through the Kennel Club or from your veterinary surgeon or pet shop.

House training is the first task with any new puppy. Puppies need to relieve themselves frequently, particularly when they have had their food or after having had a good sleep, so the first few days spent completely at home with your puppy are worth the trouble. After each feed take your puppy out where it can relieve itself on the spot you want it to use. Don't feed it outside as it will connect that with relieving itself where it is fed. Immediately it wakes up, take it outside. Never expect a puppy to go all night without relieving itself and, if it is in your bedroom, prepare yourself to leap out of bed and rush the puppy outside in the middle of the night. You can, of course, train the puppy to use newspaper which, if you are living in a flat, can be very helpful. Once the dog is over the puppy stage, if the newspaper is taken outside and put in a suitable spot, the desired habit will soon be acquired. Should you have an older Poodle from a kennel, you may find it will very often go twenty hours without relieving itself, not knowing where to go even if you take it out every five minutes. Don't worry about this as patience will finally be rewarded.

Lead training is very important. Use a long lead or tie two together if necessary. Very young puppies are usually easy to train. Just walk in the direction they want to go to start with and gradually let them feel the lead. Encourage them by word of mouth all the time and make it sound exciting that you want

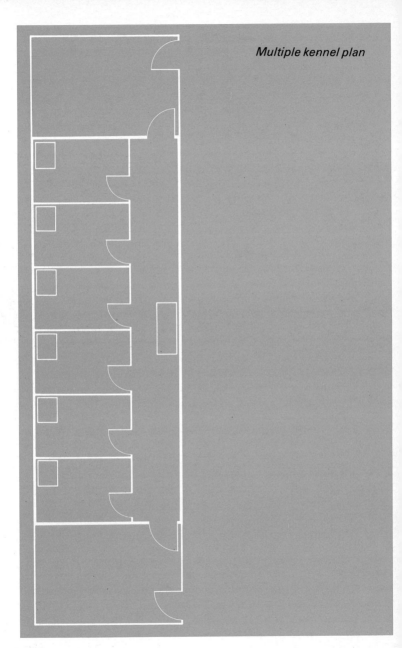

Multiple kennel plan

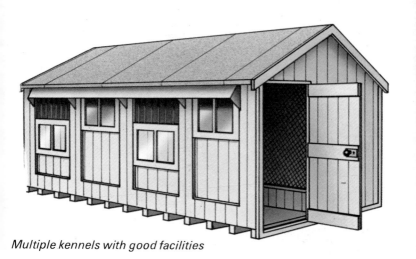

Multiple kennels with good facilities

them to come with you. Gently pull the lead so that the puppy can feel it but do not drag the puppy along the ground. An older puppy takes longer to train and will very often scream at the slightest movement and end up like a bucking bronco. The main thing here is to keep calm, ignore the noise going on at the other end of the lead and just stand still, preferably on soft ground. Once the noise has stopped, which it soon will, make a great fuss of the dog and start to walk off. If the dog sits down at the far end of the lead, squat down yourself and more often than not it will come and see what you are doing. Again make a fuss of it. Let it walk off by itself with the lead attached and, after a short time, pick up the lead and go with it. Never spend more than ten minutes at a time on this sort of training. Let the dog play with a toy, or time the training period so that the dog is fed immediately afterwards. A Poodle is an intelligent dog and will soon learn.

Once the dog has learned to walk on a lead, the next thing is to teach it to walk to heel. Usually once it has mastered the lead, the next thing it does is to pull if not corrected. So often one sees a dog pulling on a short lead and this is a mistake so many people make. Use a long lead and let the dog go the full length. Then use the dog's name and say 'Heel', at the same time jerking the lead so that the dog feels it, but not so sharply

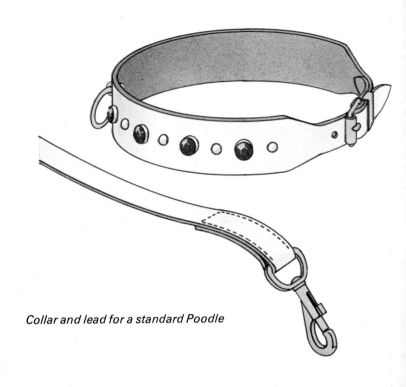

Collar and lead for a standard Poodle

as to injure it in any way. Once the dog is back, praise it. Never just pull back or the dog will simply learn to pull forward. I have not at this point suggested using a choke chain collar and do not, in fact, intend to, as these collars must be put on correctly and used correctly. A training instructor will teach this at class. Chain collars can do more harm than good if not properly used.

Teaching a puppy to sit can wait until it is six months of age when it will be able to go to training classes. To over train a puppy, particularly when it is at the teething stage, is not a good thing, particularly with the Standard Poodle which is not only teething but doing a lot of growing too.

An apricot Poodle

A silver Poodle

metal-handled coarse tooth comb

wire pin brush

Suitable grooming equipment

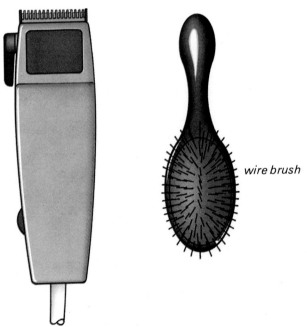

wire brush

poodle clippers

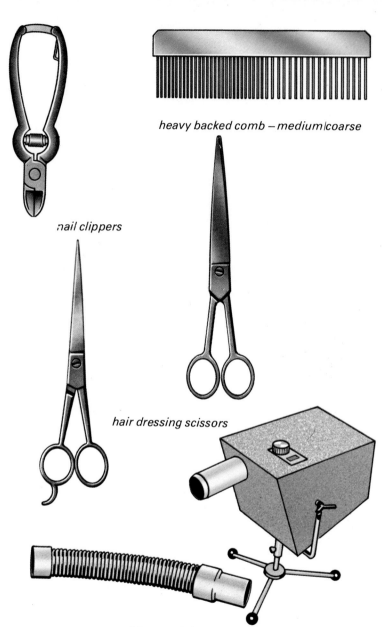

heavy backed comb — medium/coarse

nail clippers

hair dressing scissors

table model dryer, with flexible tube extension

53

A black Poodle

A cream Poodle

Grooming

The show Poodle, having been trained to lie on its side, needs very careful grooming. This is something for which time must be set aside; it is not a case of fitting it in during a spare five minutes before getting the lunch ready. Like human beings, the hair of each Poodle is slightly different. Where it says 'harsh to profuse' in the standard, profuse does not mean the length of hair but the number of hairs to the square inch. Having a big coat helps to show off a beautiful Poodle but it is also possible to have a coat which is too big, spoiling the effect.

Puppies can be shown up to one year of age in the Puppy trim; that is with face, feet and tail clipped. The rest of the coat is slightly shortened all over. At any time the dog can be trimmed with the traditional Lion trim and very often a Miniature or Toy Poodle, if it has a huge coat, looks better this way from the beginning. A Standard, having much more growing to do, can usually be left in the Puppy trim until its first birthday.

As the puppy lies in front of you with its feet towards you, make a parting with the brush down the middle of its stomach. Brush thoroughly downwards as well as upwards, using one hand to control the amount of hair which will be brushed in the next layer. A common mistake is to take too much hair in each layer so that it does not get thoroughly brushed and combed. Nor do beginners keep to a straight line, thus missing out some hair altogether. Be sure that you can see the skin through each new layer you make. Gradually, layer by layer, brush up towards the centre of the back. Then do the two legs; these need brushing out well under the armpits which usually get matted. Once that side is done, turn the Poodle over. Get the dog to lie down on the other side, the feet towards you as before, only this time its head will be facing the other way. Starting as you did before from the stomach, continue grooming until you reach the centre of the back where you left off from the other side. Next, sit the dog up with its chest towards you and brush between the front legs up towards the neck. You will find that under the ears is very likely to get matted. Then brush the top knot and the back of the neck. Groom each area in exactly the same way, layer by layer. Finally groom the ears and tail. When the dog is in Lion trim, you have not got the legs to groom but it will need its bracelets

You may wish to trim the puppy yourself for the first time.
Clip face, feet and tail, then remove the hair with scissors from
the root of the tail up to the
back of the neck then round the centre
of the tummy and down the chest

Next clip the
part that has
been cut short
with a number
5 blade in the
direction the
hair grows.

Brush out well the long hair

Trim the trousers short and under the tail and topknot with scissors

Brush the hair upwards and trim, round back of head as well then upwards over the topknot leaving a round effect.
Hold the hair of the tail and cut across

and the pack on its hindquarters combed out. All the short hair should be nice and curly, although many Poodles today seem to have that plush look which so often indicates that the coat is of the wrong texture.

A Poodle can be bathed as often as one wants. No amount of bathing, if the coat is of the correct texture, will spoil it. A large bath is a necessity for the Standard and a sink is ideal for its little brothers. No end of excellent shampoos are on the market today, most of which are obtainable from chemists, dog shops or at dog shows. Not only can you buy ordinary shampoos for Poodles but the various colours are catered for too. All are quite safe to use and free from dye or anything against the Kennel Club regulations.

The Poodle needs to be thoroughly soaked in warm water, which is quite a problem with such a heavy coat. This is particularly the case if your water pressure is not up to full strength, which means using a jug or bowl instead of a powerful spray. Do read the instructions on the shampoo bottle first and dilute it properly. Rub in the shampoo all over, making sure you have not left an area out. Now rinse thoroughly. The dog will probably need two rinses if you are

Make sure to brush right down to the skin

Make a parting across the head

Applying a rubber band to the topknot Twist the band

1

2

Hold topknot with right hand and take the band over once more, with your little finger of the left hand

3

4

not using a spray but you must be sure to get out all the shampoo. In some cases, particularly with the little ones, shampoo which has not been properly removed causes a skin irritation. Have plenty of towels ready. Give the Poodle a good rub to remove a lot of the water and then sit it on a towel on its table. If you have a hair drier, for choice two or three, the dog will soon be blown dry, with the aid of your brushing it at the same time. If you do not possess a hair drier, the Poodle can be dried in front of a good fire or out in the hot sun, but I don't really recommend either of these alternatives. Dog hair driers are an expensive item but well worth it. The driers one uses for one's own hair are not really powerful enough. It takes about three hours to dry a Standard Poodle in full coat using at least two driers. Needless to say. Miniatures and Toys take less time.

When you have learned how to groom and bath your Poodle and have partly trained it, you are ready to learn to clip. I do not suggest you should clip your Poodle out from the Puppy trim unless you have had previous experience. It is better to start by clipping a Poodle that has been previously clipped by an expert. If you ever get the chance, arrange to have a few lessons on trimming as, no matter how much one reads, it is not quite the same as seeing it done.

Use electric clippers obtainable from most grooming equipment specialists who advertise in the dog papers or sell direct at dog shows. The correct blades will be supplied at extra cost, with details of how to keep the instrument clean. Try various makes if you can, to find which suits you. At least three different blades will be required; one for the face, feet, tail and any clipping close to the skin, one for a short curly finish on the body, and one for a longer finish. You will also need suitable hairdressing scissors, varying in length of blade to suit the individual. There is a wide variety of brushes, so buy one from a specialist supplier. It is also useful to have a small pin-wire brush for removing matts. Any dog with a really matted, thick coat will need to have the coat cut off and started again. Large single matts can be pulled apart by finger and thumb and thoroughly brushed and combed. This must be done before bathing which only makes all tangles worse. You will also need very small rubber bands. The size should be such that they fit comfortably on a little finger. Otherwise one has to wind them round the hair too often which may lead to breaking the hair.

Lion trim
Brush a parting round the body before cutting the hair off the quarters to trim the Poodle into lion trim
Front leg, cut the hair with scissors just where the shaded part is, then clip in direction of arrows against the direction in which the hair grows
Trim round the coat

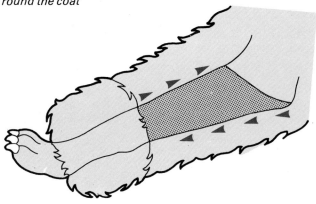

Trim with scissors in direction of arrows

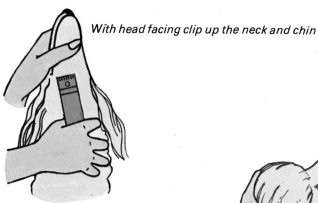

With head facing clip up the neck and chin

Holding the ears well back clip
towards the nose
Be sure to clip the skin tight

Sit the Poodle facing, hold the hair
back with left hand and clip from
ear forwards towards the nose

Hold the lips tightly back to prevent nicking the skin while clipping
towards the nose

Start off with the feet. This is the toughest part and less prone to clipper rash, although with the electric clippers of today it is rarely a Poodle gets this complaint. However, it sometimes happens when the Poodle moves suddenly, particularly when being clipped on the face. To be on the safe side to start with, apply a soothing lotion where you have clipped the Poodle close to the skin.

The Toy Poodle needs great care when being clipped. Hold it gently on the table or under the arm while at the same time grasping one front leg with one hand and gently clipping the foot with the clippers held in the other hand. It only needs two or three teeth to clip between the toes which must be separated in turn. When you have done the other front foot, the back of the feet and under the pads may be clipped from a standing position. With regard to the back feet, it depends how difficult it is to hold your Toy Poodle. It might be easier to sit down and hold the dog on your lap rather than having it standing on the table. When you have finished the feet, continue clipping the legs, providing the Poodle is in Lion trim. The hair on the front legs grows in different directions, so keep the blades clipping against the lay of the coat, and don't forget to leave on a bracelet. The length of the bracelet is determined by the structure of the dog. No two Poodles are ever clipped exactly alike. A clever exhibitor does his best to cover up his dog's faults by expert trimming. No good judge should be fooled by this but ringsiders often are!

The hindquarters of a Poodle may be clipped into various patterns. If you are aiming at narrow lines, be careful not to take too much off. Remember that the hair does not grow directly outward. It grows along the skin and then out, so one can easily clip more than one means to. The tail is very important and, if one is not used to the clippers, I would advise using scissors under the tail. If a Poodle gets a clipper rash on its tail it never seems to forget and, no matter what one does afterwards, as far as the dog is concerned that tail is always sore.

Finally we come to the face. Again this is a difficult job, particularly with Toy Poodles who seem to object on principle, especially if one is not as proficient as one should be. Hold the ears back behind the dog's head with the left hand and start clipping on the right side of the face. Clip from the ears to the corner of the eye and continue forward down the face, making sure that the skin is kept perfectly taut. Clip the neck, where again it is a matter of suitability where one starts. Turn the dog round, hold the ears back again, and clip forwards on the left side of the face. When the lips are reached, pull them gently back so that the skin is quite taut, and clip forward. Continue over the face and down the nose. A straight line or a small, upside-down 'V' can be left between the eyes. Finally, clip the hair from under the nose. The hair underneath the body can be tackled by standing the Toy Poodle up on its hind legs facing you.

When the clipping is finished, the scissor work starts. Make sure you have obtained a good pair of hairdressing scissors from the same place as you bought the clippers. Comb out the bracelets and the pack on the hindquarters and, using the scissors, trim round them both. Trim the tip of the tail and attach a rubber band to the Poodle's top knot. This needs a lot of practice, so find someone to show you if you can. Brush the hair well back on the head and make a parting roughly a quarter of the way back. Place the rubber band on your first two fingers and thumb and hold this section of hair with the same fingers while pulling the rubber band over it with the other hand. Twist the band and then draw it back again over the top knot. Make quite sure that it is not pulling in any way and causing discomfort to the dog.

The Miniature and the Standard Poodle are clipped in the same way as the Toy, but are usually easier to do. You can clip the back of the feet and the stomach with the dog lying down on its table. Lift up the hind leg and clip off the hair but be careful if the animal is a male. A clipper rash on a penis is difficult to cure, for a dog will keep licking it.

Even to show a puppy entails a lot of trimming of the coat, without which it can look very untidy. The puppy needs to be tidied up with scissors round the base of its trousers, leaving its toes showing. I might add that this is today's fashion. A few years ago the Poodle puppy was clipped up to the pisiform (that is the knob on the back of the front legs just above the pads), and the whole of the foot was trimmed of hair. Fashions in Poodle trimming change just as women's clothes do. Nowadays the hair must be trimmed round the tail and down the back of the hind legs, the aim being to give the dog an even outline all over.

To transfer a dog from the Puppy trim to a show clip, start by

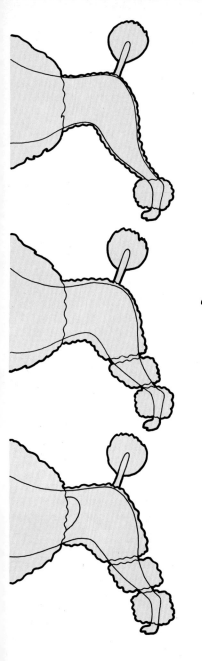

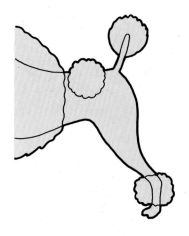

Various patterns on the quarters for the show trim

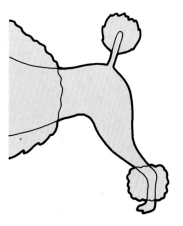

A cream puppy in trim acceptable for showing up to one year

clipping its face, feet and tail. Brush a parting all round the dog's body, roughly 2-4in. (5-10cm.) from its last rib. Trim the hair off with scissors from the root of the tail to the parting. When you can see where to clip, use a wide blade and clip over the same area. The hair must be trimmed from the legs but not as short as on the back. One leaves 2-3in. (5-7.5cm.) or more on a Standard Poodle, so that one can shape the leg bracelets and patches on the thighs, leaving a balanced look. Use scissors first on the front legs too. The bracelets from top to bottom are longer than they are wide, so cut the hair off above up to just below the elbow, and then use the clippers. Any extra hair can always be taken off afterwards, so give yourself leeway so that more can be trimmed off if necessary. Finally trim all round the bracelets. Keep combing the hair outwards while doing this for the more one combs the more even will be the result.

With the pet Poodle the choice of trim is up to the owner. Very often all the hair is taken off the neck and body, leaving trousers on the legs. But here common sense is needed. A Poodle's coat is supposed to be waterproof but above all it acts as an insulator. A Poodle trimmed too close and left out in the sun can become sunburnt or even get sunstroke. I always advise leaving at least 1in. (2.5cm.) of hair on the body. One also needs to consider whether big trousers left on the legs are practical in muddy and wet conditions.

When clipping the head, follow a straight line from top of ear to corner of eye

For a pet trim start at the back of the neck or at the base of the tail and clip the hair from the body, using a coarse blade in the clippers. One can either clip with the hair or against it, but do not be in too much of a hurry. If you push the clippers too quickly, they will suddenly stop and appear to go out of gear. If this should happen, let the clippers run without using them for a few moments, after which try them on an already clipped area using only part of the blades at a time. Having clipped the body and the chest, groom the trousers and the top knot very well. Taking your scissors, trim up and down the legs. To start with, the Poodle will look very uneven but do not despair, for with practice you will improve. It is much easier to start with a dog trimmed by an expert, and then just go over it with your clippers and scissors once a week, doing the face and tail at monthly intervals.

There are, of course, hand clippers which cost considerably less than the electric ones but which take longer to get used to. The knack of using them needs patience. Never push hand clippers. They clip at the speed with which your hands are working them. Before actually clipping the hair, work the clippers by hand so that you have the feel, as each hand clipper is slightly different. Do be sure to press the blades completely across each other, for if they are not used correctly they will soon refuse to work at all.

Correct way leaving broad wide trousers to give width

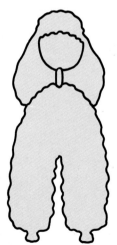

Incorrect way of trimming giving a narrow appearance

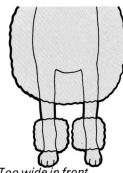

*Too wide in front
– leave more hair
on the inside of the bracelets*

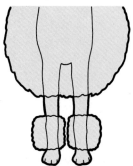

*Too narrow in front
– leave more hair
on the outside of the bracelets*

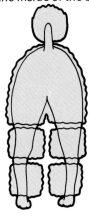

*Hocks turning out –
leave more
hair on the
inside
trimming
shorter on
the outside*

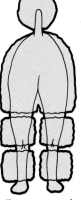

*Too narrow behind
– trim hair off from
the inside leaving
more on the outside*

*Trimming the show dog
according to his faults*

Trimming for a low set tail

Exhibiting and show training

I suppose one can say that showing dogs is a world of its own with a language of its own, a world that is getting more competitive and more expensive daily. How does one start showing one's hopeful?

In Britain there are various types of show from Exemption shows run for charity, through Sanction, Limited and Open shows to the biggest of all, Championship shows. At the latter, the very valued Challenge Certificates are on offer. To become a champion a dog must win three of these under different judges at different shows. To find where the shows are being held, buy one of the weekly dog papers, either *Dog World* or *Our Dogs,* which carry the show advertisements. The show secretary will send you a schedule, if asked, with an entry form for you to fill in. If you read your schedule through carefully, you will find definitions of all the classes and you can then choose which you want to enter. Ask advice from a breeder or exhibitor if you are in doubt.

In America show categories run from Matches to Points shows, the latter being where one can win points towards a championship status for one's dog. A dog needs fifteen points to become an American champion. *The American Kennel Gazette, Popular Dogs,* and several other dog magazines print

Transportation cage

At some shows all dogs are benched like this

lists which give the dates and locations of dog shows to be held in the near future. Entry blanks and premium lists may be obtained by writing to the secretary of whichever show you wish to enter. Match shows are more informal and dogs may be brought to the show and entered any time up to the start of judging.

There are training classes for show dogs in many areas, most of which will accept puppies from three months of age provided they have been fully inoculated. If you can take your dog to such a class, both you and the dog can learn a lot. The puppy will be encouraged to walk among other dogs. The person taking the class will act as a judge and go over your puppy to get it used to being handled. The puppy will be taught to stand correctly and the handler taught how to get the puppy in the correct position, holding the lead over the head and steadying the tail with the other hand.

I always advise anyone going to their first show to do so without a dog so that they can really take in what goes on and

The Standard Poodle should be taught to show himself

The Miniature and Toy Poodle can be shown from this angle if the handler is in a squatting position

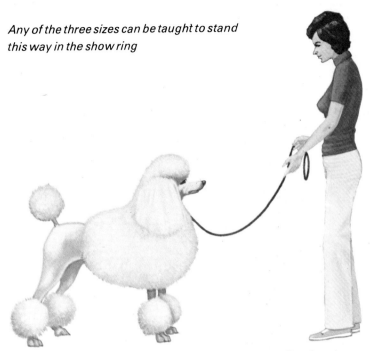

Any of the three sizes can be taught to stand this way in the show ring

familiarise themselves with show procedure. On the day you are exhibiting give yourself plenty of time. If you are tense and worried your dog will be too. You will need to take a brush and comb, a dog blanket, a water bowl and food for yourself and the dog. Benched shows are those with wooden staging where the dogs are left when they are not being judged. If you are going to one of these you will need a benching chain to fasten the dog to its own particular stall.

Most dogs are shown on lightweight slip leads when they go into the show ring. For everyday use, a round leather collar, rather than a flat one, is best, as it will rub the coat round the neck less. For the pet Poodle there is a gorgeous selection of jewelled collars and leads from which to choose. Your own clothes for a show need care too. Short skirts, low necklines and high-heeled shoes are not the most suitable dress for lady exhibitors. If you are wearing trousers, make sure that they contrast with the colour of your dog.

Let your exhibit relax and watch what is going on before

A white Poodle

getting it ready for the ring. Groom the dog well all over and finally brush all the coat on the back forward so that the hair stands out well, Comb out the bracelets and finally add the rubber band to the top knot. As the hair on a Poodle's ears grows longer it tends to get in the food and drinking water and quite often gets chewed, so it is wiser to hold this in rubber bands to protect it. Do be careful that the band grips only the hair and not the ear itself. These rubber bands, of course, must be removed before entering the show ring (which, incidentally is nearly always square!).

Most judges work to a similar pattern. I personally like to have a look at each dog first by walking up the line of dogs. Then I like to move them round in a circle, after which I like to

A brown Poodle in Continental clip

see each dog individually and get them to move away from me in a straight line and back again. Then I may choose six or seven and bring them into the centre of the ring to make my final selection. Some judges prefer each dog to move in a triangle. By watching other exhibitors and following suit, you are not likely to do anything wrong. Whether you have won or not, always praise your Poodle. This will give it confidence and it will show all the better next time.

You will hear various remarks from unsatisfied exhibitors but you should not let these disturb you. If the time comes when you hate being beaten, then the time has come to quit. Showing should be a pleasure and if you cannot feel that way about it, then leave it alone.

Table

"New" dogs (unseen by Judge)

Handler

Dog being examined by Judge

Judge

"Old" dogs (already seen by Judge in a previous class)

Table

Judge

All dogs

"Once round, please"

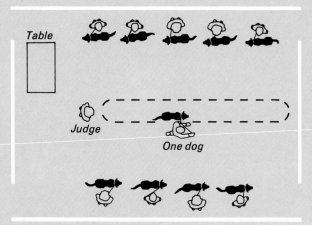

"Once up and down, please"

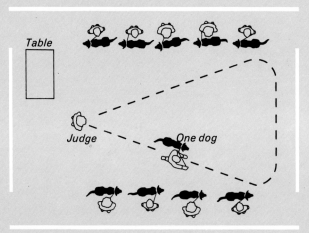

"Triangle, please"

Breeding

Do not imagine for one moment that two champions mated together will produce champions. Nothing is that easy and it is often the plainer bitch with the same bloodlines who will prove to be the better brood. A good dog will usually produce good puppies and my advice is to choose a champion dog if possible, providing he is suitably bred for the bitch.

It is a fallacy to think that a bitch needs a litter to remain healthy, or that a bitch which has phantom pregnancies will be cured of this by having a real one. A bitch can only be mated when she is 'in season' or 'on heat'. A bitch may come into season at any age from six months onwards, and thereafter at six-monthly intervals. Never mate a Poodle at her first season and indeed, if she is one of those that come into season at an early age, do not let her have pups until her third season at the earliest. The big Standard Poodles take longer to mature and it is advisable to wait until they are at least eighteen months to two and a half years old before having their first litter.

The first signs visible to the owner that a bitch is coming into season is a slight swelling on the vulva. This is followed some days later by a blood-stained discharge. This continues for some eight to ten days, after which the discharge fades to a pinkish or creamy colour. It is at this stage that the bitch will be ready to accept a dog and will often indicate by her flirtatious behaviour that she is ready to be mated. However, a bitch is attractive to males throughout the entire three weeks of her season and should be closely confined the whole of this time to prevent unwanted attentions.

It is often wiser to return to the breeder of the bitch if one needs advice as to which is the most suitable dog to use. Any sincere breeder will be happy to help, as no one should want to breed anything but the best. Once the bitch comes into season, let the owner of the stud dog know and arrange to take the bitch there. The stud dog owner may advise the best day. This is usually between the tenth and twelfth days after the first appearance of the vaginal discharge.

Once the bitch has been mated, treat her in exactly the same way as before, but remember she is still in season for at least another ten days and needs to be kept away from other dogs. It is advisable to worm her during the next three weeks, using tablets from a veterinary surgeon. At the same time let him know that the bitch has been mated and when she is due to whelp, in case you need his help. The period of gestation is sixty-three days from mating but bitches can whelp up to six days early, so preparations should be made well in advance.

During the third and fourth week of pregnancy a bitch may well go off her food. If one knows one's bitch really well, one notices a slight change of character if she is in whelp. Very often she will become a little more affectionate or slightly quieter. From the fifth week her appetite will increase and she will need some form of calcium additive to the diet. There are many excellent products on the market for this purpose, or one can use calcium lactate tablets. Care should be taken with the dosage, as overdoing it can be harmful. The meat in the diet must be increased to up to twice the normal amount for the Standard and Miniature Poodle. Toys may not be able to accept this amount of increase but all the extra food given must be of the best quality. Bitches whelp more easily if they are not allowed to get fat. Indeed fat bitches are a breeding liability, as excess weight causes difficulties both in conception and in parturition.

During the last three weeks the bitch should be introduced to her whelping quarters. Toy Poodles can perfectly well have their small families in the corner of one's room, providing all and sundry are not allowed to come and go when they like. A child's play pen screened off is ideal and a cardboard box makes a suitable bed. Leave up to 4in. (10cm.) in height at the front to prevent the bedding and puppies from falling out. Towelling makes the best bedding, keeping it flat by wrapping it round a flat piece of wood or cardboard. This is easy to wash and makes the best surface for baby pups to crawl on as it prevents them from slipping. I often think that many puppies develop joint troubles at this early age because of lack of a proper surface. Young puppies need heat, and many people use infra-red or violet ray lamps. I feel that these often cause more harm than good as few people know how to use them correctly. An overall heat, such as is provided by a radiator, with the room kept at 70°F (21°C) is adequate for the first few days, after which it can be lowered to 65°F (18.5°C). There should be plenty of absorbent paper on the floor of the play pen and a constant supply of fresh drinking water provided.

Miniatures can be treated in the same way as Toys, but as they usually have a larger litter there are more difficulties. The first three weeks are fine but when the puppies become active it is a great deal more trouble and no bitch wants to be moved out after having had a cosy three weeks indoors. The same applies to the Standard Poodle, so it is wiser from the start to have a suitable room, kennel or outhouse which is heated and comfortable. Miniatures need a proper little wooden bed about 2ft. by 2ft. 6in. (61cm. by 76cm.) and not more than ½in. (1.2cm.) off the floor. If it is any higher, one can be certain that puppies will crawl under it as soon as they are old enough. The Standard Poodle bed needs to be roughly 3ft. by 2ft. 6in. (92cm. by 76cm.). One side of the bed needs to be hinged at the bottom and slatted so that the puppies can toddle up and down with ease, again making sure that the slats are close enough so that the puppies do not slip or strain themselves.

The floor of a puppy rearing room needs to be either of wood or of a cork substance. Tiles are too slippery and concrete is a hazard to bone development. Even dog runs are better with paving slabs rather than concrete round the edges and with a certain amount of grass in the centre. Puppies should have a flooring with some resilience for I feel a lot of the bone troubles today are caused by puppies careering about on concrete and injuring themselves.

Before the litter is due, make sure that you have plenty of towels ready. You are also likely to need glucose or honey, milk, a thermometer, a hot water bottle and some styptic substance such as Friars Balsam or permanganate of potash crystals.

Bitches vary very much in their behaviour just prior to whelping. Some will go off their food, become extremely restless and dig and scratch their bedding. Others behave as normal until they start in labour. One of the surest signs that a bitch is going to whelp within the next twenty-four hours is a definite drop in her temperature. The normal temperature of the dog is 101.5°F (38.5°C) though individuals may vary slightly from the norm. Before whelping the temperature will drop two or three degrees. To take a dog's temperature, coat the bulb end of a clinical thermometer with vaseline and insert this into the rectum, holding it there for about one minute.

Needless to say, someone should be with the bitch throughout the entire whelping. Most births are normal and uncomplicated but if help is needed it will be needed quickly if

The genital organs

Dog

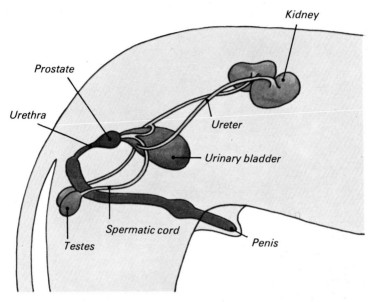

- Kidney
- Prostate
- Urethra
- Ureter
- Urinary bladder
- Spermatic cord
- Testes
- Penis

Bitch

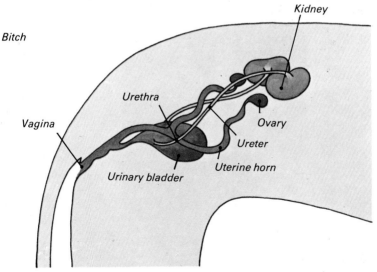

- Kidney
- Urethra
- Vagina
- Ovary
- Ureter
- Urinary bladder
- Uterine horn

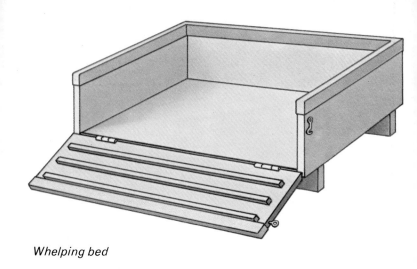

Whelping bed

Cardboard box with one side removed but leaving 1–2 in. (2.5–5cm.) in height in front to keep a blanket in

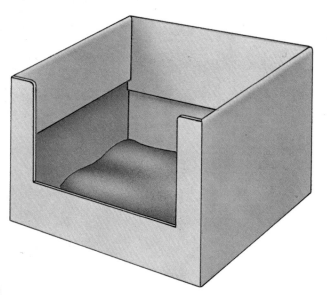

the bitch or the puppy's life is to be saved. Once straining starts, that is definite muscular contractions of the flanks and abdomen, the first puppy should be born within an hour or so. If contractions have continued for two hours without a puppy being born, then professional help should be sought immediately. Each puppy is born enclosed in a membranous sac which the bitch strips away with her teeth and tongue, biting through the umbilical cord in the process and very often eating the afterbirth. Some inexperienced bitches seem so taken aback by the arrival of their first born that their maternal instincts fail to function; in such a case you will have to remove the puppy from the membrane bag as fast as possible or it will suffocate. The umbilical cord must be broken or cut about 1in. (2.5cm.) away from the puppy's stomach and any bleeding stopped by Friars Balsam or a ligature. Rub the puppy vigorously with a warm towel. By this time it should be squeaking and the mother taking an interest, so put the puppy to a teat and encourage it to suck. Remove the soiled towelling if you can do so without disturbing the bitch too much. I like to put a well wrapped hot water bottle into the whelping box where the puppy can crawl when the next arrival is coming. I don't believe in taking away puppies as this usually upsets the bitch. After the second arrival, a drink of milk with glucose added can be offered to the mother. Once all the puppies have arrived, leave the bitch for a time to have a rest, after offering another drink. Then change all the bedding and replace with clean towels.

If there is any sign of uneasiness in the bitch, ask your veterinary surgeon to call and check up. It should be routine to take her temperature night and morning for the first four days after whelping. Any reading over 102°F (39°C) is an indication that something is wrong. Possibly an afterbirth has been retained or there is some uterine infection which needs skilled treatment immediately.

The bitch should be fed every three hours for the first three days with a light diet of fish, scrambled eggs, chicken, egg custards, sweet biscuits, etc. Raw meat may be given on the third day. Depending on the size of the litter, continue with five or six feeds a day, gradually increasing the meat and adding biscuit meal. It is wise to add a pinch of bicarbonate of soda to three of the feeds to counteract any acidity in the bitch's milk which may give the puppies diarrhoea.

On the fourth day, the puppies need their tails docking and their dew claws removed. It is very often wiser to ask a breeder of Poodles to dock the tails as to dock them the wrong length can ruin a whole litter. It is difficult to state the exact length to be left as it depends so much on the size of the puppy. With the Standard Poodle puppy about 1½in. (3.8cm.) should be left, measured from under the base of the tail. A tail that is docked too short spoils the balanced look completely. It is better to leave too much as this can be operated on later in life without undue fuss. The only exception might be where one knows there is a tendency in the family for the tail to curl over the back when the dog is adult. This is a definite fault and one would be wiser to leave on a shorter tail. Permanganate of potash crystals applied will prevent bleeding.

The mother should be taken out of earshot while the docking is done and the dew claws are removed. The puppies' nails should also be cut, and will need trimming once a week using a small pair of surgical scissors, as they can cause the mother discomfort. This is also a good opportunity to cull the litter should there be too many. Eight is the maximum any bitch should be asked to rear and six is more sensible still. The bitch can return immediately these jobs have been done.

During the first few weeks the puppies should sleep well and eat well. They should feel firm and solid to the touch. If a puppy cries a lot or feels limp there is something wrong, particularly if there are also signs of diarrhoea, which can be seen as yellow stains on the towelling. At about three weeks, Standard Poodle puppies need to be fed with scraped raw meat, a tablespoon each to start with. Gradually increase the amount and the number of feeds until by four and a half weeks they are having four meals a day. Two of these should be meat and the other two milk thickened with a baby cereal. Once the puppies start to have wholemeal bread or well soaked puppy meal added to their meat, the bitch will not need so much. As the puppies' food intake increases so the bitch's food needs to be decreased until by six or seven weeks Standard Poodle puppies should be fully weaned. Miniature and Toy puppies are weaned in the same gradual way but usually do not need to be started so soon. Always feed puppies the meat meals from their own individual dishes. It is the only way to make sure that they get their share of both food and vitamins. A place should be provided for the mother so that she can get away from her puppies when she wants to.

Puppies, like children, need a well thought out diet. There are many satisfactory methods of feeding today, from complete foods through to tinned and frozen meats and offals. All breeders have their own pet feeding methods. Personally I am a bit old-fashioned and like to feed my puppies with good, plain meat and wholemeal biscuit meal which has been thoroughly soaked. Whatever you feed your puppies on, it needs to be the best of its kind for them to grow up into healthy adults. If one intends to breed Poodles, then do study the requirements needed to rear a litter. There are far too many people doing it haphazardly with no thought at all as to correct feeding. The diets here are a guide rather than a must, for one must use common sense and adjust accordingly.

By the time they are eight weeks old, Standard puppies will be eating daily 12oz. (350g.) meat plus puppy meal, vitamins and 1 pint (½ litre) of milky food. This will be divided between four meals. Miniatures will need half this amount and Toys about a third. Never underfeed a Toy puppy thinking this will keep it small. Its adult size is dictated by its breeding background. The four meals a day routine should be continued until three months when one meal can be dropped. By six months two meals a day should suffice but of course the quantities must have been increased. Standards will need from 1-1½lb. (½-¾kg.) meat daily up to a year of age, reducing to ¾-1lb. (350-450g.) daily when they are fully mature. Miniatures will need up to ½lb. (225g.) meat daily by the time they reach a year, reducing to about 6oz. (175g.) as they become adult. Marrow bones are excellent for dogs to chew but never give anything smaller that can splinter. Vitamins are needed throughout growth but do be careful about the required quantity. It is so easy when one is in a hurry to fling on spoonfuls when a pinch or two is all that is required.

There are two other considerations when rearing a healthy litter. All puppies have roundworms and need worming. This should first be done at about four weeks and then again twelve days later. Always be careful to give the correct dosage. All puppies also need inoculating. Some veterinary surgeons will start this at eight weeks while others prefer to wait until twelve. If you are selling your litter, make sure that the purchaser is given full information about this.

Six weeks is the time to take a good look at the puppies and start to choose which ones to keep for the show ring. Stand each puppy up in turn and really study the bone structure. Compare each puppy with the others and if there are two similar, then go for the one with the most outgoing temperament. You cannot tell for certain at this age the eye colour or whether you will get a level mouth with a full set of teeth. You can see such faults as long backs, thick heavily boned skulls, short or badly set on ear leathers, and short necks. Look for correct shoulder placement and tightly knuckled up feet (not so common in Toys and Miniatures as in the Standard). A low set tail not only spoils the top line but very often means badly made quarters. A tail which curls over the back is also a fault. Do not choose to keep a shy puppy as these can be heart-breaking to show.

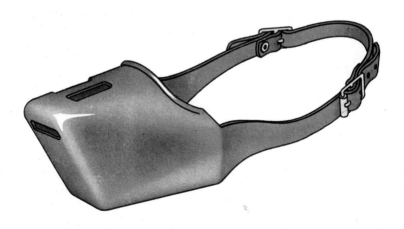

Muzzle of moulded plastic which can be sterilized and used as an anti-rabies measure

Health

On the whole Poodles are a hardy breed and do not suffer from any more troubles than the average dog. Ear infections should be watched for, as the long ear leathers covered in hair prevent air reaching the ear canal. Unless the ears are kept clean and free from hair inside, they can soon become infected and ulcerated, needing a great deal of treatment. This can end up with the ear having to be operated on, which soon clears up the trouble but does spoil the appearance.

The two glands situated on either side on the anus and known as the anal glands can become filled with an evil smelling thick liquid. This is usually caused by too little roughage in the diet. The symptoms may include the dog dragging its hindquarters along the ground or suddenly turning round and madly chewing the area of the tail. A verterinary surgeon will be able to relieve this condition by expressing the fluid.

There are various inherited abnormalities which have crept into Poodles from time to time and which should never be bred from. One such condition is entropion, an abnormality where the eyelids turn in so that the lashes continually rub the eye, causing pain and discomfort. One cannot detect this condition until the puppies are nearing three months of age when a continual watering of the eyes will begin to be noticed. This condition can be operated on, but no genuine lover of any breed would dream of continuing a line with such a fault. Another inherited eye condition is P.R.A., Progressive Retinal Atrophy, where the victim becomes blind at an early age. There are no symptoms that are noticeable to the unqualified until the dog's sight fails, and nothing can be done. This appears to be more prevalent in Miniatures and Toys than in Standards and serious breeders have done their best to eradicate it. Hip dysplasia and slipping patellas are both joint deformities causing lameness and eventual arthritis. It is these inherited abnormalities which are the most serious hazards in nearly every breed. Although one does one's best to eradicate these distressing complaints, one must always be alert for any re-occurrence or for anything new cropping up.

Poodles are not prone to skin infections but eczema can cause a great deal of worry. This can be caused by wrong feeding or by an allergy. The skin irritation causes the dog to chew and scratch until there is a wet, sore patch of skin. You should get professional treatment quickly as Poodles take an age to grow hair after any skin injury. To make it worse, the coat grows back a different shade. In whites the new hair grows in an orange patch, in silvers it is black, in browns a darker brown, in blacks a darker colour with a different texture, and in apricots the new hair grows in dark brown patches. This eventually rights itself but it will be seen that the sooner skin infections are cured the better.

Fleas and lice love a thick coat like a Poodle's so one should always keep a look-out for these insects. A special shampoo is the best way of dealing with them.

The elderly Poodle needs extra care and consideration. As the dog gets older the sight is not so good as it was, the hearing not so sharp, the joints a little stiff and the coat a little thinner. Do not let the dog get wet without drying it thoroughly. When it is being bathed and trimmed, do not expect it to stand up for too long. A bath takes a lot out of an old Poodle, so it will need plenty of rest. A warm, woolly coat and a macintosh add to the dog's comfort, but do not expect it to walk too far. Food should be given little and often. If the dog has always leapt on to a chair, put a stool in front so that it can do it in two stages, but never, of course, let on that you have done it to help. Stairs are a problem; carry the dog up if necessary, for it would hate to be left down if it has always slept in your bedroom. Like humans, some Poodles grow older more quickly than others, and an occasional check on heart and kidneys is a good idea. When the time comes to part, do not let it linger too long, for no dog should have to suffer that indignity.

A healthy Poodle is a dog full of life and fun who loves its food and eats well. A sick Poodle more often than not starts off by becoming quiet, going off its food, perhaps vomiting, coughing, walking stiffly and generally looking miserable. One should never waste time treating the Poodle oneself, even if the symptoms seem minor, such as being sick two or three times or having diarrhoea. Ask for veterinary advice, for many dogs have died through lack of early treatment, and a Poodle's life is too short as it is.

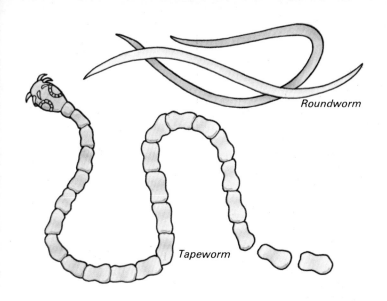

Roundworm

Tapeworm

Adult flea

Biting louse

Engorged female tick

Mite (microscopic)

Sucking louse

Parasites

READING LIST

Bowring, Clara, and Munro, Alida. *The Poodle.* Popular Dogs Publishing Co., 1953.

Dangerfield, Stanley. *Your Poodle and Mine.* Barrie and Jenkins, 1954.

Sheldon, Margaret, and Lockwood, Barbara. *Poodles.* W.G. Foyle Ltd., 1957.

Sheldon, Margaret, and Lockwood, Barbara. *Clipping your Poodle.* W.G. Foyle Ltd., 1962.

Sheldon, Margaret, and Lockwood, Barbara. *Breeding from your Poodle.* W.G. Foyle Ltd., 1963.

Hopkins. *New Complete Poodle.* Howell Book House, 1964.

Rogers. *Poodles in Particular.* Howell Book House, 1967.

Stone, P. *Clipping and Grooming your Poodle.* Gifford, 1970.

Miller, Harry. *Know How to Clip a Poodle.* The Pet Library Ltd., 1971.

Glover, Harry. *The Batsford Book of the Poodle.* B.T. Batsford Ltd., 1974.

Glover, Harry. *Poodles.* Viking Press, 1975.

Poodle Council Yearbook, obtainable from any Poodle Club in Britain.

BREED CLUBS
Poodle breed Clubs are so numerous, world wide, that it is not a great help to list them. To find the address of your nearest breed club, contact the Kennel Club.

KENNEL CLUBS
The Kennel Club, 1, Clarges Street, Piccadilly, London W1, England.
The American Kennel Club, 51, Madison Avenue, New York, NY 10010, USA.

DOG MAGAZINES
Pure Bred Dogs. American Kennel Gazette. Published by the American Kennel Club.
Dog World, 22 New Street, Ashford, Kent, England.
Our Dogs, 5 Oxford Road Station Approach, Manchester 1, England.

Index

Distributors for
Bartholomew Pet Books

Australia

Book Trade : Tudor Distributors Pty. Limited, 14 Mars Road,
Lane Cove 2066, New South Wales, Australia

Canada

Pet Trade :   Burgham Sales Ltd., 558 McNicoll Avenue,
Willowdale (Toronto), Ontario, Canada M2H 2E1
Book Trade : Clarke Irwin and Company, Limited,
791 St. Clair Avenue W., Toronto, Canada M6C 1B8

New Zealand

Pet Trade :   Masterpet Products Limited,
7 Kaiwharawhara Road, Wellington, New Zealand
Book Trade : Whitcoulls Limited, Trade Department, Private Bag,
Auckland, Wellington, or Christchurch, New Zealand

South Africa

Book Trade : McGraw-Hill Book Company (S.A.) (Pty.) Limited,
P.O. Box 23423, Joubert Park, Johannesburg,
South Africa

U.S.A.

Pet Trade :   Pet Supply Imports Inc., P.O. Box 497, Chicago,
Illinois, U.S.A.
Book Trade : The Two Continents Publishing Group Limited,
30 East 42nd Street, New York, N.Y. 10017, U.S.A.